For my Mom, Truly, who was a gifted
writer and an inspiration to me.

"I say follow your bliss, doors will open for you that wouldn't have opened for anyone else." – Joseph Campbell

"Love can provide greater bliss than any wealth or possessions and is capable of transforming a person's entire being in an instant." Author unknown, from Love Quotes by David Baird

"At the touch of love everyone becomes a poet." – Plato, from Love Quotes by David Baird

A Note to the Reader:

In February of 2010 I was signed up for a Qi Gong class on "Love," when I found a poem I had written on December 30, 2007. I decided to bring the poem to read, and share how it came to be written: *I awoke from sleep that December morning, "singing" the poem! I went to my computer and wrote out the poem in less than 15 minutes. This was the first draft of the poem "My Goddess."* The poem and its story were well received by the "Love" class members and they wanted copies. I promised to find it on my computer and print out copies; meanwhile thinking about sharing my poetry and myself. What happened next was quite bizarre. I looked for the poem on my computer, the title was there, but when I opened the document, it was BLANK! No huge problem, since I had my much-folded hard copy. So I retyped the entire poem into my computer, and saved it many times. Along with this strange computer glitch, I was getting messages in my dreams, that if I did not share this poem, it would not be there. So I made the copies for the class members and shared my poem. This was the beginning of a spiritual journey I continue to experience—as the words are channeled through me. I am a conduit for the poetry and its messages.

Although I've been writing poetry since I was a teenager, most of it was never shared, just saved here and there in spiral notebooks. In the late 70's, as a young mother I wrote several poems about my children and my thoughts, and submitted them to a ***Poetry Anthology, Lyrical Voices* (1979)**. When the publisher asked for money to get my poems published, I could not afford that at the time. However, they liked some and published one poem titled *"Reflections,"* and I purchased one copy of the book. Around this same time (1977-1979) I also began studying reincarnation, experiencing Reiki, past life regressions, and healing massage, as I explored my spirituality, after a move to Oregon. My poetry writing was put on hold for many years, as I raised children, worked part-time, worked full time as a draftsperson, then went back to college, and finally moved back to Minnesota in 1993 to teach Middle School.

I retired from teaching in 2009 and chose to renew my passion for studying reincarnation and spirituality. After reading a book by Brian Weiss, I looked for a past life regression therapist to help me understand some new connections I found in this lifetime. The two regressions sparked past life links with family and others, reaffirming my spiritual path toward unconditional love. I wrote *"Pink Cloud"* immediately after the first regression. I was shown my purpose: to share the message of LOVE with the world. Then *"Love Encompasses All"* was written the day before the second regression. From that point on the poems flowed through me, sometimes very rapidly, channeled through me onto my computer. What I have discovered is that there are no coincidental meetings or events; everything that happens in your life is part of a larger plan and purpose.

Supported by my family and friends, I continue to write and share my poems. To help continue my spiritual growth, I attended my first I CAN DO IT! Conference in San Diego, shortly after my mother passed in May of 2010. While there I met a representative of Balboa Press. My self-publishing adventure was about to begin. I want to thank so many Hay House authors for their wisdom and gifts of teaching that have enlightened me, challenged me, and awakened me through books and workshops. I attended another I CAN DO IT! Conference in Toronto in May of 2011 continuing to learn and grow in remarkable ways.

My poems reflect my journey; they are about love and bliss, love of self, love of others, love from God and the Universe. The poems also reflect deep soul connections ranging from the never-ending love of past life loves to present day discoveries of unconditional love. In this book of poems I am sharing my love, my process towards bliss, and myself. The words, rhymes, and rhythms come through my heart and soul, channeled by the cosmic consciousness. I hope my words inspire you to find you own love and bliss. It was not by chance that you picked up this book. Enjoy!

Wynnie
St. Paul, Minnesota
November 2011

CONTENTS

SECTION 3:   Living And Loving With Bliss

FIND YOUR BLISS

SOUL POEMS CHANNELED AND WRITTEN

BY

Wynnie

SECTION 1:

Discovering Bliss

MY GODDESS

I have a goddess within me, no need to scream and shout.
I have a goddess within me, put away your fear and doubt.

My goddess is pretty, and smart and thin.
She is there inside me, if I look within.

My goddess can heal, and help and care.
My goddess is here now, and everywhere.

She is like my Angels, protectors are they.
My goddess relays what the Angels say.

I have a goddess within me; she's there to watch over me.
I have a goddess within me, I wish I could be like she.

My goddess is kind, resourceful, and bright.
She is shining inside me like a bright light.

My goddess is truthful, honest, and nice.
She can handle all problems, without thinking twice.

My goddess is strong, athletic, and swift,
But she is my goddess and that is a gift.

How can I repay the energy source,
For giving me such a wonderful force?

I have a goddess within me; now what am I to do?
I have a goddess within me; first I will say, "Thank you."

Next I will count all my blessings, mom plus grandkids make five.
I have a goddess within me; it is so great to be alive.

More blessings I have in my children, my loves, and friends do count too.
My goddess holds closely each memory of all we did, say and do.

One more verse before the cool finish, insightful as it may be.
I love the goddess within me, and hope she won't ever leave me.

But here's the truth to this riddle, it came to me through head and heart.
I am the goddess within me, bright, carefree, and swift like a dart.

I am the goddess within me, it's time to scream and shout.
I am the goddess within me, it's time for me to come out.

My goddess wants me to share this, be it a story, poem, or song.
Thoughts being shared with others are what goddesses do all day long.

PINK CLOUD

Floating gently on a vaporous cloud of pink
And white tinged with sparkling blue.
Love is surrounding me in every form,
I am me, I am she, I am you.

Embracing arms of Love caress me,
Cloud-like energy speaks to my mind,
Warmth and safety, Love and contentment,
With the "earthly world" left behind.

Higher energies surround me with Love,
I am cradled, a rocked child, a soul.
Learning is telepathically shared,
With Love encompassing the whole.

Pink cloud of energy and Love so grand
Stay with me, caress me, please do.
Healing Love penetrates my wholeness,
Loving me, loving she, loving you.

POETRY SAYS IT ALL

What is Poetry? A rhythm of life,
A rhyme in all those times of strife?

Feelings coming through the words,
Gently flying by like the birds.

There is a beat, a cadence set,
Which poets struggle over yet.

Muses help with creative bursts,
Even if you write blank verse.

Subjects vary the world over
One stands out, go ask your lover.

Poetry is written for meetings,
Music lyrics, and card greetings.

Poetry uses words in rhymes
Expressing bliss and joy at times.

Be proud of your thoughts here and above
Write a poem for someone you love.

YOGA WITH SARA

I meditate as the mountain, great and tall and strong
Breathing to the rhythm of my very own heart song.

Volcano breath heats up my lungs and my beating heart,
Fire, lava, spewing ash, all part of nature's art.

Look and form a book, silently we speak in prayer
Opening layers, closing again soul layer upon layer.

Squatting into moon flowers, a hue of blue at night
Closing now at sunset, opening up at the first light.

I view and scoop the sunflowers; in the wind they blow.
Soaking up the sunshine, yellows waving as they flow.

Turning slowly becoming warrior, armor-clad and brave,
Warrior one, then warrior two, survival's what I crave.

Standing tall, I am the tree, with waving leaves so green,
Balance wavering, think like a tree; please pardon as I lean.

Walking forward like a giant, oaken roots unearthed.
Swinging right then left around, tottering with my girth.

To the floor we go as cobras, music charms our way,
Hissing, slinking, listening, but there's no prey today.

Spinal twist feels good to do, eyes closed I feel the light,
First we stretch out to the left, and then we do the right.

Forming animals: exhale for cat with spiky hair and spine,
Inhale gently into cow. Where's the grass he left behind?

Oh to the sleeping child we go, peacefulness — don't nap.
While in this pose I'm dreaming of children in my lap.

I become a pretzel, salty and twisted and brown,
Twisting pulls my muscles, holding longer brings a frown.

In staff pose legs and toes stretch out, torso bending too.
Sole to sole, bound ankles hold — I hold, I breathe, I do.

Meditation ends the class, thoughts calm, I want to stay,
But now relaxed and muscles eased, I go with NAMASTE!

LOVE ENCOMPASSES ALL

Love enriches and love enhances.
Just as dancers love their dances.

Love's for friendships, love connects
Men and women, vets and pets.

Love cuddles you and love surrounds
With kisses, hugs, and soothing sounds.

Love completes, does not deplete us,
There is always more to treat us.

Love gives hope, love gives joy,
Just like a new little girl or boy.

Love grows stronger from our heart,
Love grows even when we're apart.

Love brings yearnings for true bliss
A wonderful feeling you cannot miss.

Love is thoughtful; love is blind.
To each of us true love is kind.

Unconditionally we strive,
Love is needed to stay alive.

Love has stages and love matures.
When love finds us, love endures.

Love encompasses all you see
From humans to the bumblebee.

MASSAGE BLISS

During a session of hot stone massage, relax enjoy every minute;
Smoothness and heat are unusual — technique is not very different.

Imagine yourself being nestled, heated hands, heated stones, there goes stress.
Carefully easing away tension, the therapist knows how to do this.

Lying comfortably and resting your eyes, you're cradled in peaceful bliss.
Hot stones massage muscles with caring hands, leading you to healing
success.

Trusting is important you see, sleep if you want, or rest being aware.
Muscles are softly treated to restorative and stimulating care.

Drifting away as scented oil renews wellness, relax now in silence.
Your caregiver works the magic, arms and hands sliding with eerie
guidance.

Lose yourself in bliss, being mindful and open, communicating, too.
Hot stone massage gives insight and wonder with healthy benefits for you.

Joy, rapture, pleasure, well-being, and happiness are synonyms for "bliss."
A soothing massage from smooth kind hands, warmed by hot stones,
provides me with this.

MICHAEL, MY LOVE

Your name is so popular, even an Archangel uses it.
Your love is so right, as I continue to encompass it.

Long ago we met as young people enriching our minds.
Your kiss made me tremble, what did you have in mind?

Separation came before we were together long.
Engagement and marriage followed right along.

Parenthood amazed us with our little girl and boy,
How did all those years fly by, so full of joy?

Raising kids, working hard, my Michael did his fathering.
Kids' growing from pre-school through college was life altering.

Loving you was always a pleasure, ecstasy was so fine.
Michael loves with passion and grace; he's all mine.

Moving, changing, life does happen without oppression.
Minnesota docs helped find relief from your depression.

Cats filled our lives as grown children lived on their own.
Loving kittens connected to us for years until full grown.

Successful children made us very proud to be their parents.
We bought our house in Minnesota, avoiding the high rents.

Love continues to be strong, my Michael you are so warm,
My job keeps me busy while you keep me safe from harm.

Children marry, and then came the grandbabies four.
We are so loved and blessed, with family galore.

Retirement for you was hard, but your support was so dear
To me as I took one more year, to finish up my career.

My retirement brought joy, and pain, as disease challenged you.
My love for you was very strong; healing love was given, too.

Reflecting back on all our love, all your strength and actions
Have kept me growing, encouraging me to follow my passions.

I love you Michael, with all my heart, we are connected by our souls
With love and caring enriching our lives, we will reach our goals.

AI CHI IN THE POOL WITH HOLLY

Space yourselves for meditation,
This pool of water's deep and warm.
Ask for clarity and clear space
To rid your practice of all harm.

Begin with CONTEMPLATING now,
In water smooth, without a breeze.
No waves upsetting our FLOATING
As arms gently flow up with ease.

Breathing is essential for all,
Inhale up and then exhale down.
Eyes closed, hands underwater move
Heads nod and smile, never to frown.

UPLIFTING water, low to high
Our meditative being calms.
Shifting gears we are ENCLOSING
Water pressure resists our palms.

Now bring energy from the deep,
ENCIRCLING under the surface,
Then down again and circle back
Counterclockwise, keep the slow pace.

SURROUNDING hugs the water so,
Energy balls ease tensions, slow.
NURTURING brings love so joyful
To you and all, enjoy the glow.

SHIFTING uses leg energy,
Arms flow side to side intently.
Good energy in, as bad goes out
Waters caress very gently.

Our arms begin the GATHERING,
Water, energy merge, no sound.
FREEING moves you around your space
But still few ripples can be found,

FOLDING water, how is that done?
Slowing down to a sculptor's pace
FLOWING stirs up the water more,
Cross then open through tranquil space.

Spiritually feel ACCEPTING
Taking time to heal with the love.
ACCEPTING WITH GRACE glorifies
Energy sent us from above.

ROUNDING follows as legs stretch out
As backs round, hands are not apart.
Turn to the left repeat all three
Clarifying with mind and heart.

BALANCING challenges each one
As right leg tries to flow-on through.
Then back, as other foot holds still.
We try again, the left leg too.

Pacing exercise is healthy
Mental pictures help to recall:
Gently SOOTHING smoothes the water
Like a massage can soothe my all.

Ai Chi practice is almost done,
ENCLOSING we replay today.
Then CONTEMPLATING reappears,
Hands fold to chest for NAMASTE.

I AM AN ORPHAN

Today my mother crossed over into heaven
Leaving my brother and I all alone.
We miss her dearly, as she was the best
We know she will never really be gone.

What is it like to be an orphan?
No parents to care for or about.
Mother loved us unconditionally and
Was someone we never did doubt.

We can take care of ourselves, okay
With spouses and families so strong.
Mom lived to be 96 years old.
It was nice to have our mother so long.

We are not orphans who run wild in the street
Like all the girls in *Little Orphan Annie*
Or those who have so little to eat,
Like *Oliver Twist* and all his cronies.

We are older than "orphans" as most people think,
But my bro and I are still orphans, no doubt.
We will follow Mom's wishes to have a party,
And enjoy living our lives with her spirit about.

EYES

Once a brown-eyed beauty
I rollicked in Tahitian sun.
My love had blue/gray eyes
Or were they more blue/green?

Hazel eyes enchant me
In this earth life today,
As those eyes turn to match
His shirt choice of the day.

My mom's very light blue eyes
Sensitive always to light.
Kindly caring through her years
Loving all was her delight.

Grandkids four, two with blue eyes,
Older two with eyes of brown.
Filling life with many joys,
From soccer games to princess crowns.

Today caring eyes intrigue me,
So light, so clear, so sharing.
I know you from our lives past.
Your eyes are calm, not glaring.

My eyes are blue, darkly edged.
My blue eyes just love to smile
Although that makes more wrinkles.
Look into my eyes a while.

POETRY INSPIRATIONS

Speakers who care,
Authors who speak of love,
Souls present in the now,
And always God above,
Inspire me.

Friends both new and old,
Teachers who are bold,
Lovers who ignite our passion,
Books and crystals sold.
Inspire me.

Children, grandchildren, moms
Inspire us to love beyond our means.
Writers and publishers inspire, as
Soft beds and nighttime shadows lean.
Inspiring me to dream.

SOULMATE MEMORIES

Lilting music gently touching my soul
Seeking a connection to love,
Seeking connections to wholeness,
Seeing connections to oneness.

Feelings are intense, connections are felt,
Longing for love while I'm dreaming,
Longing for caring joyfully,
Longing for those we call soulmates.

Love surrounds, love intoxicates
Remembering feelings so strong,
Remembering lives rich and long,
Remembering me, you, and more.

Joy is mine, recalling past lives.
Loving is what revives the dream,
Loving as your body hugs me,
Loving unconditionally.

SOUL SEARCHING

Within us all there lives our soul.
It helps us care and grow.
It helps us know and love.
It helps us ebb and flow.

Our soul is what controls our heart.
Love comes from the soul.
Peace comes from the soul.
Our soul, it makes us whole.

Without our soul we are empty.
Empty as a shell with no animal.
Empty as a glass without liquid.
Empty as a car with no driver.

Knowing our soul helps us find purpose.
Purpose to love and know love,
Purpose to be and do wonders,
Purpose to enlighten from within.

Our body surrounds the soul.
Our heart listens to the soul.
Our soul lives on forever,
Even if our body cannot go on.

Earth's purpose is emanating
Through souls with hearts so kind.
Listen within, find your soul.
Sharing love isn't hard to find.

Watch your ego, meditate.
Calm your mind and reach within.
Soul searching can be done.
Soul searching is for anyone.

I LOVE MYSELF

I love myself; no critic am I.
Find fault with me, and I may pout
Or laugh and sing with joy and love.

I love myself; no judge am I.
No one is better or worse than I.
I am a friend of few or many or all.

I love myself through times of pain
Or heartache caused by fear or shame.
I look to love to forgive and set me free.

I love myself; I love to dance
Ballroom or rock and Salsa, too.
I'll dance to music when I get the chance.

I love myself and I love you.
To love me back could be the rule.
Unconditional love is ours — be brave.

I love ME! I love YOU! Love is all there is!

SECTION 2:

Appreciating And Sharing Bliss

GRATEFUL FOR LOVE

I am grateful for love. Love that I receive,
And for all the love I give out to others.
I'm grateful for the challenges of love, too.

Although conflicts are frustrating to us all,
I'm grateful for the opportunity to
Resolve or dismiss challenges with my loves.

Travel experiences help me to share
My love and friendship with new acquaintances.
The beauty of our country revives my love.

Feeling the sun's warmth and the wind in my hair
Makes me grateful for the Earth and for God's care.
Travel challenges help me to grow and learn.

I am grateful for unconditional love,
As I work on spiritual enlightenment
With all those I love here on Earth and above.

I AM GRATEFUL FOR LOVE!

KNOWING

The knowing in your heart, the tugs, follow directions.
Be sensitive to others, test your intuition.

Strong feelings in your "gut," urgings flowing from your heart,
Voices telling, as if reading someone else's part.

Dream memories, daydreams, too, add to the psychic flow.
If you're thinking too much, knowing fades or doesn't show.

Go inside, listen to yourself; hear all those thoughts.
As memories touch your mind, know the past without doubts.

Knowing and intuition are the same you will see,
As mind, body, and soul connect universally.

ENERGY

Electromagnetic energy controls Earth.
Electromagnetic energy surrounds you.
Energy connects us, one soul to another.

Energy is exchanged from rocks to living things.
Special connections are made by soul energy.
Energy surrounds us, just as Love can ground us.

Energy can be positive or negative.
People give off different "vibes" and potency.
Learn to recognize and take in good energy.

Energize yourself, bring in something positive.
From negative, protect yourself with healing light,
And let crystal stones tend to your safety tonight.

Meditate and listen to your own energy.
Listen to your soul's response to a stranger's "vibes."
Heighten your senses for picking up on clues.

Intuition, sensitivity, and soul work
Are helpful as you tune in to the Earth's array.
Be mindful, energy and spirits are one today.

LOVE   LISTEN   ENERGIZE

GRATITUDE

Gratitude is pouring out of me,
Like water from the falls.
Unconditional love surrounds me,
As if a child with dolls.

Using intuition, being brave,
It was worrisome at first.
I am so grateful for my strength,
WOW! I could climb Mount Everest.

Being grateful for all love
Can be a daily gift alone.
I now understand the "we,"
All beings combined as one.

Light is bursting forth from me,
Energy embraces, touches me.
Gratitude, love, compassion,
Belong to you and me with glee.

The Universe is wise and good
As God works his wonders daily.
I wish more humans got the drift,
And repaid kindness fully.

One final note on gratitude,
Giving to others isn't profound.
We always "reap what we doth sow,"
So plant your love into the ground.

HEALING HANDS

Friction can create a warming,
Transferring heat, very thermal.
Healing touch creates channeled heat,
Energy is universal.

Massaging hands create friction.
Energy brings the channeled love
As healing flows by conduction.
The energy sent from above.

Hands get warm as heat is transferred
But when hands get hot you can feel
Healing coming through your skin,
As your therapist helps you heal.

Relax and meditate in bliss.
As tensions are released for you,
Caring energies are at work
Through therapist's hands to renew.

INTUITION

Riddles in time, were known before, and are now sought.
Intuitive signals flow as energies are held,
Logic and analysis fly out the window,
Bringing deep connections, as all loving souls meld.

Perceptions of knowing, deeper feelings, and love,
Knowledge of ancestors through my past and future,
All overlap, swirling around my head and heart.
Is <u>this</u> intuition or just my conjecture?

Deep in meditation, heaven's urgings abound,
Spirits speaking, conversing, not judging, no rush.
Intuitively sensing all there is to know
At this one moment in time, don't say a word, hush!

Knowing when, knowing how, with loving and sharing.
Intuition rejoins that which has been apart.
Love energy fuels intuition, WE ARE ONE.
Changes in perception, heal the world, heal the heart.

CHANGE

Feelings trembled in my being.
Change was happening in this life.
To some it seemed so trivial
The news to me cut like a knife.

Why did I have feelings like this?
I was sad, I felt pale and drained,
Like limp spaghetti in a dish.
You were moving on, I felt strained.

"Change causes grief" some seemed to say,
I gather "grief" was what happened.
I had to take some special time,
And grieve for hearts we had opened.

Love does not stop, no matter what.
I know this change did briefly test
The feelings deep within my chest,
As I wished you the very best!

Music and my poetry helped,
As healing made its way through me
And opened up the blockages.
Time helped, too. "Butterflies are free!"

FLY   CONNECT   LOVE

℗

JOY

JOY comes from within and expresses itself through smiles,
Laughter, and merriment; true JOY is within your heart.

Ballroom dancing gives me JOY each time I dance I fly
Around the room with a smile, happiness is my guide.

Therapeutic massage gives me JOY, healing touch with
Warm hands and oil delight the senses of my smooth skin.

Receiving good news from old and new friends gives me JOY.
Knowing others are well and happy makes me joyful.

Loving brings JOY to others, to you, and grows within.
Learning is joyful in this lifetime of soul searching.

Grandchildren bring merriment; it's theirs to always share.
Don't waste childhood moments, feel JOY, feel laughter, feel love.

Music is heart lifting, full of creativity.
The rhythm and sounds lead to "toe-tapping" joyfulness.

Finding JOY is not that hard if you look and listen.
Meditate in nature and find JOY within your soul.

Sunshine, raindrops, and bright rainbows bring JOY to the skies,
Flowers radiate beauty from the ground, nature smiles.

Hugs bring JOY, warming each body with heat energy.
Connections are made as souls send love through each embrace.

JOY is pure love energy expressed in loving smiles.
Create JOY, invest in love, and smile your woes away.

TREASURED GIFTS

Look to nature for wonders and glee
Like a small child, be open and free.

Listen to music for ease and beat
And dance — if you can get on your feet.

Give hugs and cuddle those you hold dear,
Feel their good energy flowing here.

Be in the moment, quiet your thoughts,
Enjoy the gifts the spirits brought.

Look skyward for awe and openness
See the stars in all universes.

Touch, hug, hold hands, and smile from your heart.
Treasure all the gifts your eyes impart.

Find the gifts in experiences.
Be the one who gives love — and dances.

MY LOVE

I have enough love for all.
No need to worry, my love.
My heart is open due to
Soul connections from above.

Unconditional love reigns
When all people look within.
Earth is working toward this feat
I am chosen to begin.

My purpose always has been
To show love to all others.
I was hesitant and closed,
I grew through past life wonders.

Now I feel love for many,
Friends, family, and for you.
No hesitation, love flows
Through me from heaven's clouds, too.

Love is joy, and peace, and light.
Thoughts of loving surround me.
I'm made to share all my love,
One day you'll finally see.

Through all my lives, you will be
A great true love, unending.
Love grows, love stays, and love shows
The wonders of our being!

BE   LOVE   HUG   TOUCH   CARE

ARE YOU MY ANGEL?

Your kindness speaks so well of you,
Your silent listening prevails.
Your energy is special, too.
Are you my guardian angel?

Angels help and encourage us.
Angels hear our every thought,
Healing happens with angels, too.
You must be the angel I sought.

Angels know what will soon occur,
Their knowledge is so very pure.
You are psychic like an angel.
When will you let me know for sure?

Angels choose to be on earth now,
While energies are changing so.
Angels heal us and help bring peace.
I embrace the love Angels show.

Love is felt from all kind spirits,
Love is given from God on high.
Love within is the best to find,
Unconditionally we try.

So be my Angel, thank you much!
Trusting is important for this.
I hope you plan to tell me soon
And help me find the clues to bliss.

SEASON OF CHANGE

Changes are happening to all
As summer weather turns to Fall.
Leaves fall, winds blow, clouds fill the sky.
Nature's cycles are riding high.

Healthy change with exercise and
Eating well, then muscles expand.
Body thins, looking good, inside
And outside, feeling good with pride.

Soul searching brings changes for you,
And sometimes for those you love, too.
This enlightens both heart and mind,
Brings peace and gratitude so kind.

Love opened my heart; changes came.
Love is my purpose, without shame.
Love surrounds and I glow with joy,
Love connects me, time to enjoy!

But with love comes heartache or more,
Friends move on, parents cross over.
Feelings may wane or stay the same,
Unending love connects twin flame.

The Universe figures it out,
And helps us grow, if we have doubt.
Be patient, love, and do believe
God is here to help you receive.

Change is good, change is positive,
If you listen, it is relative
To where you are and how you love.
Love's all around, here and above.

Embrace the love within your heart
Give love to others, that's your part.
Grow and change, be grateful to those
Watching over you, head to toes.

COCOON

Once a caterpillar fuzzy,
Eating leaves and living free.
No worries, but prey I could be.

Caterpillars are born to change,
They're waiting for their catalyst
To help them form their chrysalis.

Spinning my cocoon of silk,
It wasn't easy, not so quick.
A cocoon was formed dark and thick.

While in cocoon, my heart yearning,
Were you my path to the learning,
Safely, caring, and concerning?

Inside my cocoon, I dreamt
A life that was different.
I was not an on-ground pet.

Time has passed, the seasons changed.
It was safely prearranged,
I would soon be emerged.

The cocoon (with comfort and love)
Helped me to change so much of
Myself, through you and above.

Now it is time to emerge,
But I fear an open charge
Into a world so very large.

Your care is my safety net.
I depend on you, and yet
We could fly just like a jet.

Will I break out of that skin
Of brown cocoon, very thin?
Open cracks — see light again.

Here I come — I'll reappear
With some hesitance and fear.
Change is tough; will you be there?

Slowly, thoughtfully with grace
I can see your welcoming face
Spread my wings, I'll fly to space.

I soar, as butterflies are free.
Joy is mine; fly high with me.
We both can fly, and both just be.

FLY   FREE   LOVE   BE

WHO AM I ?

Am I a teacher, no longer with young students,
Trying to find people to teach all my knowledge?

Am I a mom seeking approval from my children
And getting unconditional love through grandchildren?

Am I a daughter, with parents on the "other side,"
Hoping they are looking down with love and pride?

Am I a metaphysical scholar, reading about connections,
Love, the Universe, intention, and the oneness of it all?

Am I a married woman with needs and desires,
Living in the moment, trying to stay grounded?

Am I a female being, living in the present
But dreaming, and longing for past life energies?

Am I an unconditional lover of many,
Sharing love with the world through my poetry?

Am I a ballroom dancer longing for a partner
To dance away the hours and find more joy?

Am I a yoga student looking for meditation,
And stretching to link the body, mind, and soul?

Am I a patient of physicians looking for
Solutions to wellness through tests and medicine?

Am I a client of healing therapists who use
Non-traditional methods to revitalize me?

Am I a grateful student of the Universe,
Trusting God and hoping I am on the right path?

Am I an eccentric person in some other's eyes,
Living and believing in my own realities?

Am I an Earth Angel, helping Earth in unique ways,
Working with others to bring prosperity to all?

Am I all of the above, at this moment in time,
Living, aging gracefully, loving with heart and soul?

YES, I AM ALL OF THE ABOVE, striving for oneness.
I am here for a reason, as all of us are now!

AGING

In this wondrous world
There are places where
Time and space do not exist.

When we look at our bodies
We know that time changes
The physical parts of us.

Wrinkles form on faces
That seemed so young
Such a short time ago.

Joints ache and stumble
As our minds push our
Bodies to work harder.

Hands, soft as babies' skin
Become dry and dotted with
Spots that mark the aging.

Gravity pulls on tissues
So beautiful breasts now sag
And belly droops without Lycra.

Yet there is beauty within.
Love shines through aging eyes,
Lines erase for a moment in time.

Our souls see this and smile.
See the beauty in you and me.
Love makes all things possible.

LOVE   SMILE   BE

BE WELL

Smile, feel free to change.
Change the illness from within.

Unleash the tools you have
To heal yourself, today.

Find the joy within the illness,
Listen to your heart and soul.

Archangel Raphael is there, too.
Just ask, he will help you heal.

Green light means Raphael is there.
Be calm, breathe in your wellness now.

Be strong and brave and bold.
Don't give in to fear or pain.

Love is being sent to you today
To help you heal from inside out.

Follow the love, to conquer all,
From common cold to cancer cure.

BELIEVE   SMILE   BE WELL

THE UNIVERSE

Although it started with a BIG BANG,
The Universe is not a criminal or a bad thing.

The Universe is beautiful with galaxies and stars,
Asteroids, Solar systems, and planets, including ours.

Colors real and imagined fill the Universe with flare.
Reds and yellows and blues, with black and white everywhere.

The Universe is all encompassing and shimmery,
Full of Love energy, it is God's luminary.

The Universe is a thoughtful place where souls live
In bodies of beings, searching and trying to give.

Caring love dwells within Earth's uniqueness,
Emphasizing the grandeur of God's ONENESS.

Trusting the Universe is one of our hardest goals,
Especially for Earth's expressive and growing souls.

Listen to your SOUL as Universal energy revives
Guiding you now and in all your future lives.

Goodness, love, beauty, energy, and YOU
Create reality and make up the Universal crew.

TRUST   LOVE   LISTEN   GROW

FOLLOW YOUR PURPOSE

Once you find your purpose, be true to your own soul.
Meditate with mindfulness, working toward your goal.

Directed by your spirits, angels, and your guides,
Forget your ego — move forward, swallow all your pride.

Don't worry if your purpose is not clear as yet,
Know that you have a goal, which is not hard to get.

Looking for purpose is not the way to find it,
Go within; listen for clues amidst the quiet.

When you find your special plan, you will know its call.
The heartfelt joy will capture and enhance your "all."

If now or if tomorrow, patience is your plan.
Recall the Universe will hold you by the hand.

Problems may arise, but clarity will appear.
Listen to the message as blessings challenge fear.

Take baby steps to reach and grow beyond it all.
Breathe deep, bury expectations. Don't rush, don't fall.

With all your actions stay on the ball; relax,
Give of yourself. Smile. Find joy in every task.

Now spread the word, choose love and kindness as the rule.
Be grateful, work with joy, and love will see you through.

WHEN GOD GIVES YOU LEMONS

Breathe your troubles away
Turn clouds into rainbows.
God's giving you LEMONS
To see what you'll do now.

Be glad for challenges,
Progress is being made
Soul work is being done
You're on your way, today.

Through LEMONS we learn life
Lessons while here on Earth.
The lessons teach of love
Today and since your birth.

When winter is lousy,
Cold wind with rain or snow
Smile and be thankful for
Those driving skills you know.

When the summer wind gives
Us higher temps and storms,
Be glad you have LEMONS
To make cool drinks when warm.

Please choose the positive
When given LEMONS, too.
Love and kindness will shine
Through all you say and do.

In spring and summer stir
A batch of lemonade
From the LEMONS you get.
Smile for all God has made.

I LOVE MY BODY AND SOUL

Thank you body for holding up so well.
You are always ready in the morning,
Even if I stay up so very late.

You are such a good friend to remind me
When I need to slow down or rest or seek
Some medical or spiritual guidance.

Body, you're reliable, creative,
And colorful. (I love my reddish hair!)
My skin is soft and smooth, and loves massage.

You are resilient and intelligent,
Petite in height. You are beautiful to me.
Your greatness is connected to my soul.

I'm so grateful for such a precious soul.
My spirit is loving and delightful.
I feel your comfort within my body.

The love and caring of my spirit helps
My body to eat right and exercise.
Body and soul love to dance and share love.

Spirit, you bring the twinkle to my eyes.
You bring the joy to my heart when I dance.
You connect God and me for only good.

Thank you soul for opening me to love.
Thanks to all who helped me open to love.
Goodness is mine. Smiles are mine. Love is mine.

BLISSFUL BLESSINGS

Blissful
Feelings
Happiness
Joy
Hiding in corners, being so coy.

Enjoyment
Pleasure
Gratitude
Goodness
Finding daily, when you're blessed.

Personal
Friendships
Loving
Aglow
Bringing you together, ready now?

Wanting
Hoping
Praying
Remember
Let blessings happen; don't ask for more.

Be Open
To Love
Create
Attract
You have sweet bliss, no need to retract.

SNOWFALL

My soul loves the beauty of a snowfall
The cold scent of winter, chills I know.
But those perfect little flakes keep coming
Down, down, into a giant pile of snow.

Each snowflake is unique, just like people.
Flakes assembled together make white lakes
Of lovely cold snow piled high, all one.
Our souls are one, like a pile of snowflakes.

We shovel, we push, and compress the snow.
We make snowballs, snowmen, and snow angels here.
The snow makes our cheeks red and skin so cold.
But something is cool and comforting there.

Blizzards blow the snow making it hard to see.
Carefully we travel out in the white,
Driving is difficult when the snow blows.
Try not to fall, enjoy the white delight.

All the trees are covered, squirrels dig for food
Beneath the layers of snow. Birds feed hard.
Most animals feel the need to sleep
With the mountains of snow in the yard.

Cozy snow caves can be very special
With rooms carved out of a mountain of snow.
Warm and safe, scented with brisk cold air.
Meditation brings me to that cave now.

SECTION 3:
Living And Loving With Bliss

MUSIC FILLS MY HEAD

When music fills my head with joy
Daydreams fill my head with you.
The lyrics usually say it all,
Just lay with me as lovers do.

Rhythms, rhymes, and sounds connect
With vibrations of each soul.
We listen, talk, feel, and hug
As music swirls to make us whole.

Music seems to harmonize with
Our dual energies and heartbeats.
Rock to pop, and old to new, heals
And speaks to us anew. Souls meet.

Favorite songs repeat once more
Lilting lyrics, passions reveal
The love we had so strong before.
Hearts opening to have it all.

Time has passed since love so fine
Claimed our souls to our delight.
Our blissful passion, full of life,
Now in our reach, yet out of sight.

Please love me now, when you recall
Our spirit energies of old.
Do not leave me alone to sing
Fond melodies out in the cold.

SOULS SHARING LOVE

We're in harmony, at peace, in tune.
Our music rhymes, as melodies rise.
Energies match, as our eyes twinkle,
Souls sharing love, it is no surprise.

Friendship encompasses passion, as
Skills and gifts we share in unison.
Mellow conversations enlighten,
Meanwhile dreaming, mesmerized as one.

Tranquility's found when we're alone,
Near one another with hearts so kind,
Waiting for those sweet moments in time
As love surpasses, all thoughts unwind.

Energies connect as fingers touch,
The heat is passed through one another.
Breathe, feel, and hear as our souls agree,
Please listen well, forgive each other.

Bonds unbroken, love is forever
Here in earth time and learning now.
The Universe controls all roles
While we play out the unending show.

Bathe me in your tender caresses,
As I release my musings to you.
Capture all the zest and love we've known,
It's in harmony we breathe anew.

WISDOM

Thank you for sharing your wisdom,
In little quotes or conversation.
You are wise, and good, and kind,
Which shows through demonstration.

Wisdom comes in many forms
From ancient voices to current trends,
From inner soul work to ego thoughts:
In love, in caring, and making amends.

Inner wisdom may be difficult to find.
But access it well through heart and soul.
Your wisdom can be your best friend,
Are you wise beyond your years, and whole?

We are born with so much unused wisdom.
Our soul memories know so many things.
Oh, to be able to tap that memory now,
Accessing soul love could be mind-boggling.

Enjoy your wisdom by sharing it often,
With friends, colleagues, and those you love.
Wisdom helps you make a difference
In this life and beyond, here and above.

Dig deep and find the wisdom that is yours,
Your inner workings know that love is there,
Intelligence, senses, intuition,
Are yours to use, wisdom makes you aware.

FREE HUGS

Feel warmth from the body next to yours.
Warm arms surround, a gentle embrace
Filled with caring, sharing, and kindness.
Hugs bring love in and to the surface.

Humans, animals, and plants love hugs.
Pets love the brushing with the hugging.
People feel the warmth — like cuddle bugs.
Hugs are preferred to people shrugging.

Love is transmitted through many touches.
Energy is all around, feel it now
Through a hug, or a kiss, or just a look.
Give hugs freely, it's a joy. You know how!

Free hugs are unconditional moments,
When we feel the universe surround us,
With love, and light, and heavenly goodness.
You'll be amazed when you give free hugs.

Hugs can last longer than you imagine.
Recall your last hug, fondly received
Feel the heat of the love energy
Passed on to you; you were not deceived.

Start hugging yourself; let arms surround
Your gentle breasts, smile with love anew.
Close your eyes and imagine hugging
Someone special; what thoughts enthrall you?

Keep feeling the warmth, the love, the caring.
Send that good energy to those you love.
Remember that hugs are free to give
To everyone guided from above.

HUG   LOVE   BE

WHY?

Why do I feel so complete in your presence?
You stirred my soul and made my heart blossom with love.
My head spins with thoughts of past and present times.
My body trembles with excitement and playfulness.
Why all this inner turmoil with you, now?

Why does your touch elicit such wonderful energy?
Your caring is loving, kind, and warm.
Your body language shows uncertainty and courage.
Your words, carefully chosen at times,
Make me feel as if I'm in a novel.

Why was I drawn to you like the pull of a magnet?
Like a moth to a flame, I flew in openheartedly,
Unaware of any dangers or fears.
Where reality takes second place to all else,
I try so hard to stay grounded and in-body.

Why are we still together, are we spiritually connected?
The strange quirks of fate, only the Universe knows.
Music awakens past longings, and feelings
Between the human energies called you and me.
I feel healing love energies and reflect them back to you.

Universe please guide me, please guide you though all this.
Talks we have, intimacies we keep, a life we've shared.
Why is unconditional love difficult? (I work at it each day.)
Clouds of light protect us; Chakras open us up to knowing
What the Universe has in store for our future love.

YOU ARE FORGIVEN

Forgiveness seems to some to be a passing thought or act,
But true forgiveness comes from within, from your soul in fact.
It is an attitude to carry you through when you're blue,
To forgive and forget the wrongs someone has done to you.

You can forgive your parents for lacking parenting skill,
But if they gave love from their hearts, you're better off still.
Forgive your children; challenges helped their spirits to grow;
Benefiting you, in loving ways only your souls know!

You should forgive your soulmates from all your lives far past.
Some loved and left you over time, knowing love would last.
"I will love you always" were the very last words avowed.
Soul love does go on, with selective memories allowed.

Sharing past loves in the present, may not always work well,
You recall past feelings, others choose the present to dwell.
Mentally you send them love, with forgiveness in your heart
To let them know you love them still, and know you'll never part.

LOVE   FORGIVE   SMILE   BE

WINTER LANDSCAPES

Sitting in a house so warm, looking out the window.
All I see is snow so white, it's winter here you know.

Away from city lights and streets, near the rural towns,
You'll see white bark on birch trees, not hearing any sounds.

This calm, peaceful scenery can make you almost gasp,
Know this majesty unfolds to give you what you ask.

We are here now to renew, to write, and hone our craft,
Listen to the soul within to know you're on your path.

Winter landscapes do contrast the outside with the in,
Comparing the brain to the soul, cold air to warm friend.

Gratitude, joy are mine for this worthy gathering,
My poems are enriched by those who are connecting.

Call it universal love; call it winter weather,
For me this moment brings our journeys all together.

CONNECT TO MOTHER EARTH

Spirits speak to us each day
Heal the earth they seem to say.
Mother Earth is in rough shape,
Her feelings hurt, was it rape?

The waters that she shares with us,
Are clean and dirty, and cause much fuss.
We try recycling here and there
Humanity's still not aware.

Lumber jacking, and mining, too
Have taken what she gave to you.
Please plant a tree, or a shrub,
Reclaim the land we cannot scrub.

Connect to mother earth by touch,
She feels your gentle hands at once.
Plant a garden; sow the seeds,
Don't forget to pull the weeds.

Give the Earth a chance to flourish
Otherwise we all will perish.
Be grateful for all that's granted
To people of this blue planet.

SAVE THE EARTH

HAPPY TOGETHER

Spending time with you I'm happy.
Your humor sometimes brings on glee.
In our special times together
Bliss may depend on the weather.

Concerts, movies, picnics, parks,
Even when it is after dark.
We go out and have a good time
Even eating out is sublime.

Conversations can be so real.
But sharing feelings is ideal.
Sometimes we don't see eye to eye,
We're good listeners when we try.

I hope your comfort zone is reached,
When we adventure to the beach
Or visit friends and relatives,
Who bring harmony to our lives.

Working together finding joy
Planning things that we both enjoy
Will keep the grumpy times at bay,
Remembering it's time to play.

RELATIONSHIPS

Purposeful relationships, such as spouse and child,
On Earth's plane help souls learn to give love sweet and mild.

Soulmates do connect with us in this earthly life.
Bringing us bliss, love, passion, and some karmic strife.

Working through these connections is our purpose here.
Learning how to love and care is our task, my dear.

Friends appear who encourage our thoughts and wishes.
Souls we know join us here, just like schooling fishes.

Even neighbors, friend or foe, help you find your path,
Through sharing, caring, and forgiving without wrath.

Spirit guides are guardians who can listen well.
Angels and the Universe guide us through the swells.

All relationships embrace doing joyous acts,
While teaching us to connect through our soul in fact.

Enjoy your family, friends, and soul-linked lovers.
Smile and bring your joy to everyone who matters.

LIVE   LOVE   SMILE   CARE

NEVER DOUBT MY LOVE

Never doubt my love, because it is true —
Coming from my heart and soul right to you.

Never question my feelings — they are real.
My heart knows truths intuitions reveal.

Don't doubt my caring for others and you,
I care in ways that show my love is true.

Never stop to question the things I do,
Time will reveal all, when God's ready to.

Sharing love poems about lovers past,
Or spirits in time, doubt need not be cast.

Believe in my love for you, now and then.
Forget your questioning, I know you can.

Think joy and love for me, and family,
All you want will come to pass, easily.

JOY   LOVE   HOPE   FOREVER

FIND YOUR BLISS

What gives you the most joy? Look within your heart
Find your precious gift from which you dare not part.

Breathe in rapture and ecstasy, and care
To all those who give you bliss and keep them near.

Unconditional love makes you smile and glow.
A remarkable feat, feeling this you know.

Happiness is yours when you do what you love.
Share your gifts — get inspiration from above.

Finding all who care, awakening your bliss,
Sharing such joy and love. Yes, you can do this.

Once you find true bliss, share your love, laugh, and play,
Keep love with you always, God will lead the way.

SMILE   JOY   LOVE   BLISS

BEING MARRIED FOR 45 YEARS

Time has a way of passing through troubles
Without a care.
Memories strive for goodness and blessings,
We were born to share.

Meeting very young, saying vows at twenty,
Were we ready?
Togetherness and separations seemed to pass
Quickly, my buddy.

Our baby added to our joys and thrills,
I was a young wife.
Sailor you were far away, then home again
Was there strife?

Fast forward now, we live in our town,
Two kids for us.
Grandparents galore, helpful and not,
But what's the fuss?

Keep going west young man — find your dream.
So lovely and green,
Mountains and ocean tempt us on to grow,
A beautiful scene.

Loving, learning, growing, and parenting
Where did the years go?
Jobs change; careers are forged,
Together or apart we grow.

Friends we have always been, and will be,
That's the secret key.
Companions now with cats and you,
Marriage is what you see.

Doing, going, arguing when money's low
But closeness still.
Retirement, incomes lower, taxes hover,
Stress makes you ill.

Illness, depression, changes threaten
Our togetherness.
Parents pass on; children live far away.
Is this our test?

Travel opportunities awaken senses, and
Happiness is there.
Being together through ups and downs.
Are you aware?

Cuddle bugs we are, be it bed or chair.
Loving arms about me.
Kisses daily, hello, goodbye, and all
Those in between.

Loving happened naturally, we were in sync.
Problems need to flee,
Years of fondness keep us strongly caring
Never doubt, just be.

SOUL LESSONS

Learning lessons from our soul
To grow into the light,
We try our best on Earth's plane
To do what's always right.

We try to find our purpose
Sharing love and joy.
Caring completely without conditions,
You are not a decoy.

We've been here many times before
For hard work and for play.
Sometimes our lives are positive
Sometimes we go astray.

Love is unconditional.
Friends to one and all,
Show you care in words or songs
Or make that one phone call.

Be grateful, share joy and bliss,
Dance, listen, and sing.
Don't run and hide from the fun,
Unless your arm is in a sling.

Don't be afraid, show you have talent,
Be very brave and gallant.
Give and get "abundance" now,
Sharing from your wallet.

Thinking only thoughts like: "be happy."
Ignore the TV news.
Your reality will treat you well,
Dreaming while you snooze.

LOVE   LAUGH   PLAY

ZUMBA BLISS

There is a new craze in town,
Have you tried it yet?
An exercise and dance in one
It is Zumba — don't forget.

Curves machines are good for you,
With music playing, too,
But when you add Zumba beat
It all seems so brand new!

The moves are like the Rumba,
Salsa, Merengue, and Swing.
High-energy workout, time flies by
As arms go up and your hips zing.

I've heard many women love it,
(But guys can learn the dance.)
On Friday nights at Curves near by
Our partying is not by chance!

Cumbia and Charleston dances
We learn parts of each in line.
Using Curves machines to workout
We are done in half the time.

Latin music sets the rhythm
You're singing, smiling, with a shout.
Blissful fun is happening for all,
That's what Zumba is all about.

KEEP IT POSITIVE

When problems bring you frustration,
And you feel your energy droop,
Think like a child, quite positive
Then start to twirl a hula-hoop!

When some people make you nervous,
Don't stress, don't pout, don't cry or scream.
Look for the positive in them.
Send them love, and offer ice cream.

When money worries get you down,
Ask the Universe to help you.
Abundance checks, less spending can
Help you jump out of the hole, too.

Keep it positive when you can.
Put on a smile, never a frown.
Don't crawl back into bed depressed,
Get up, find joy and walk to town.

Pass on your joy to all you meet.
Thank them using your gratitude.
Tell them how you beat the doldrums,
Share how you changed your attitude.

KEEP   SMILING

I BELIEVE IN ME

I believed I could fall in love,
So at quite a young age, I eloped.

I believed I could be a good mother,
Two wonderful children are my reward.

I believed I could do well in college,
When I was young and older, I succeeded.

I believed I could draw homes to sell,
And worked at drafting for many years.

I believed I could coach girl's softball,
Enjoyed every minute, All-Stars showed me.

I believed I could relearn, and teach
Science and math, and I did until I retired.

I believed in being a grandmother, too
Unconditional love from grandkids comes through.

I believed I could learn to dance
Joy is mine as I Salsa and Tango at last.

I believed in my writing about love and bliss.
I prepared my poetry to self-publish.

I believed in reincarnation and twin souls
Love is all there is, here and above.

I believe in me, I believe in you, I believe in love.
Love keeps the Universe going.

SHIFTING TOWARD BLISS

Living with your heart open
May not happen when you ask.
Letting love in, loving back
Is your most important task!

When your own shift will happen
Is already meant to be.
Blissfulness will follow as
You find your path: one, two, three.

Peacefulness is genuine
When your life goes with the flow.
Love will be the key to bliss
Let creativity show.

Personal growth, self-esteem,
And happiness will follow,
As you reach toward your purpose
By embracing all love now.

Expect a quantum moment
When the shifting does appear.
You'll be ablaze with feelings
As bliss overcomes your fear.

SUSPENDED TIME

I gaze into your eyes
At that moment in time
I become young again,
As the world stops, you're mine.

Joy is ours, my heart beats,
It beats of love so true.
A never-ending love,
We are one, born anew.

Standing there suspended,
Breathing in your essence,
Remembering our past
Lives of love and lessons.

Don't awaken me from
This blissful timeless trance,
Transfixed on your kind eyes
My soul newly enhanced.

Mindfulness calls us back.
How much time has passed by?
Are we still embracing?
With warmth our bodies sigh.

Back to reality,
Grounding ourselves in time,
To part for now knowing
Our connection is sublime.

STORMY NIGHT

Awakened by storm noises, I hear the thunder boom,
As cracks of lightning flash and illuminate the sky.
Constant rumble shakes my house and me within it now.
Are messages being sent, dispersed within rain clouds?

Long ago when storms appeared, the Greeks believed their gods
Were fighting, hurling lightning bolts at one another.
When other ancient people heard the crash of thunder,
They believed Thor's hammer was pounding through the heavens.

What metaphors today bring some peace to those afraid?
God is not an "angry god" fighting others above.
Now "Love" is all there is to shoo people's fears away,
Besides learning the science of weather and big storms.

Temperature imbalances, cold and warm air collide
Making rain pour down upon my windowpane tonight.
Ions, plus and minus, bring us flashing lightning now.
Which in turn creates the thunder as the bolts rebound.

Rain may be a metaphor for God sending love on
To loving humans and those who may have closed their hearts.
The bright flashes of lightning with its thunder booming
Awaken sleeping folks, bringing joy and love with rain.

Those I love, here and far away are within my thoughts.
The weather strikes a chord, bringing changes to the air.
Do I need time to reflect on feelings I covet
Between the earthly loves and those who are in spirit?

Spirit loves share blissfulness no matter what I do.
Earthly loves bring challenges and karma to undo.
They all are important for life lessons big and small.
Will lightning flash into your heart bringing openness?

"Love is all there is!" so why was I awakened too?
Perhaps to get me thinking this is an "act of God,"
Or to write poetry to share the bliss from above,
While the Universe sings to us: "It is raining Love!"

MUSICAL BLISS

My heart is filled with love,
My spirit fills with joy,
As blessings surround me
And music lifts my soul.

Cloudy days seem sunny,
My body fills with heat,
As warmth and light shine from
The love I feel inside.

Energy waves caress
As words, sounds, and love are
Transmitted from music,
As I sit here dreaming.

Creative musicians
Sing melodies that lift
My consciousness to a
Higher level of joy.

Music revives my love
For mankind and the earth,
Spirits, angels and guides,
Loved ones here and above.

My gratitude is huge,
For gifts of love and bliss.
Sending thanks to all who
Share love through their music.

LISTEN   LOVE   SING

WORDS

Your words sweetly written
Go straight into my heart.
I'll save them there until
We understand our part.

When our lives collided
No clues were given out,
About the connection
That love would bring about.

Spiritual love is rare
In cases such as ours.
Settings bring out caution,
Boundaries are not bars.

Talking, sharing, caring
Continues to enrich
The meaning of our words
As we navigate this.

Familiar souls now
Embodied as strangers.
Trying to re-connect
With words on these pages.

Please, hug me once or twice
Again to let me know you feel
The linking souls we share
Are helping us to heal.

Acknowledgments

This poetry book could not have been completed without the love and support of many people. First of all, love and gratitude goes to my husband Michael, the person who helped me become the person I am today. He has been very helpful with my work, and is also a past-life connection. Love and appreciation to my two wonderful adult children, their spouses, and my four beautiful grandchildren who continue to teach me all about unconditional love. Thanks to my brother, James who has always accepted me for who I am, with love and understanding since we were very young. I also want to thank my parents, and sister, Laurie who always encouraged me to be the best I could be, no matter what I did. Now they are encouraging me from the "other side."

Throughout my writing process many people have been helpful, supportive, and encouraging:

Denise Gunderson, an extraordinary Qi Gong practitioner/healer, who initially read and encouraged my poetry writing in its early stages. Thank you for inviting me to join classes on Love, Intuition, Pendulums, and the Body, which educated and enlightened my spirit and mind. Denise, thank you for helping me to recognize my capabilities in many areas.

Edwinna Sackariason, massage therapist, friend, mentor, and sounding board when the poems kept coming through me. Edwinna helped me find my deepest truths and soul connections. She has supported me from the beginning of this journey and before, healing and teaching me. Thank you, Edwinna, for helping me put all the connections together and explaining the revelations I did not understand.

Karen Carr, life coach, friend, an editor of these poems, without whom this finished product would not be so cool. When I wanted to attend my first conference, Karen said, "I'd like to meet you there." We were on our way to the I CAN DO IT! Conference in San Diego where the connection to Balboa Press was first made. Thank you, Karen, for all of your support and insight.

Emily Moore, friend, teacher, environmentalist, who desired "a road trip companion" to bring a crib (her father had made) to California to be there to greet her first grandchild. This was the transportation and catalyst that took me to California in May of 2010 and to my first I CAN DO IT! Conference. Thank you, Emily, for listening to me, my poems, and the music of TRAIN all the way to California.

Maggie Chula, spiritual counselor, past life regression therapist who took me on the voyage through two past lives which changed this lifetime for the better. During those sessions, I learned about divine past life connections to souls here today. I also found my purpose to "share love with the world." Thank you Maggie, for helping me open myself to this journey of love.

Cari Koebke, sister-in-law, friend, former teacher, who listened and encouraged me as I embarked on this journey of discovery and writing. We share a strong interest in many Hay House authors, exchanging books with each other regularly. Thank you Cari, for attending the September 2011 Wayne Dyer event with me.

Patty Petersen, friend, editor, and the person who suggested having three sections for this poetry collection. She also helped edit the book proofs. Thank you Patty, for your expertise and encouragement.

Rebecca Metz, a businesswoman, technology trainer, and friend, who is an organizer of "writing retreats" for women. Karen Carr suggested I join her at one of the retreats. Now after three retreats, I gratefully thank Rebecca for the wonderful experiences and time to work on my poetry.

Maria Shaw-Lawson, astrologer, intuitive, and author, helped me gain clarity and direction on my spiritual journey through readings and encouragement. Maria's Psychic Fairs in Roseville, Minnesota also put me in contact with some other psychics and intuitive readers, who continue to encourage my progress.

All the staff at Balboa Press who helped me along this self-publishing journey. Mollie Harrison encouraged me, when I had doubts about sharing my poetry with the world. Mara Rockey, Lacy Chupp, Jennifer Slaybaugh, and Emma Gliessman for being extraordinary contact people (Check-in and Publishing Services Associates.)

Hay House authors: Louise Hay, Brian Weiss, Wayne Dyer, Sonia Choquette, Denise Linn, Gregg Braden, John Holland, Doreen Virtue and others, who have inspired me through their writing, speaking, and workshops. These authors helped teach me about reincarnation, soul love, and spiritual connections, which influenced my choice to embark on this spiritual writing journey.

Appreciation and thanks goes to all my caregivers: my acupuncturist, doctors, and massage therapists who keep me feeling healthy and happy; to all my instructors of dance, yoga, water aerobics, Ai chi, Qi Gong, Curves, and Zumba who keep me motivated and ageless during this journey. Gratitude goes out to friends who channel spirits who are continually guiding me with love. I also want to express gratitude to God and my spirit guides, angels, soulmates, my muse, and the universal cosmic consciousness for love, guidance, inspiration, and your gifts during this wonderful on-going adventure.

Thank you to everyone who has encouraged me to share myself and give love to the world through poetry. Your support is truly appreciated.

Alphabetical Index Of Poems